As If a Song Could Save You

WISCONSIN POETRY SERIES

Sean Bishop and Jesse Lee Kercheval, series editors
Ronald Wallace, founding series editor

As If a Song Could Save You

BETSY SHOLL

The University of Wisconsin Press

Publication of this book has been made possible, in part, through support from the Brittingham Trust.

The University of Wisconsin Press
728 State Street, Suite 443
Madison, Wisconsin 53706
uwpress.wisc.edu

Gray's Inn House, 127 Clerkenwell Road
London EC1R 5DB, United Kingdom
eurospanbookstore.com

Printed in the United States of America
This book may be available in a digital edition.
Library of Congress Cataloging-in-Publication Data

Names: Sholl, Betsy, author.
Title: As if a song could save you / Betsy Sholl.
Other titles: Wisconsin poetry series.
Description: Madison, Wisconsin : The University of Wisconsin Press, [2022] | Series: Wisconsin poetry series
Identifiers: LCCN 2022013231 | ISBN 9780299340742 (paperback)
Subjects: | LCGFT: Poetry.
Classification: LCC PS3569.H574 A9 2022 | DDC 811/.54 23/eng/20220—dc19 LC record available at https://lccn.loc.gov/2022013231

In Memory, Always—
John Douglas Sholl

But you—let the light encircle you.
  —OSIP MANDELSTAM

One murky island with its barking seals
Or a parched desert is enough
To make us say: yes, oui, si.
　—CZESLAW MILOSZ

Contents

Acknowledgments

Heartfelt gratitude to the editors of the following magazines where these poems first appeared:

Aquifer: The Florida Review: "Elegy with Bats"

Brilliant Corners: "*Ugly Beauty*"; "After the Keynote Address, the Drive Home"; "Thomas Merton Experiments with Meditations on Jazz"; "Slow Night at the Piano Bar"; "Bargains"

Crab Orchard Review: "Starlings"

Field: "*Miserere Mei, Deus*"

Four Way Review: "Widow, Walking"

Hunger Mountain: "Missing Person"

Image: "Thinking of Jonah at the Children's Museum"; "Corcomroe Abbey"; "Ladders of Paradise"

I-70: "Transmigrations"

J Journal: "The Daffodils"

Literature and Belief: "The Birthday Party"

Maine Sunday Telegram: Deep Water: "The Caterpillar"

Michigan Quarterly: "*Knot*"

New Ohio Review: "One Step"

Numero Cinq: "Bear"; "Everest"; "*Happy, Happy, Happy*"; "*There Is a Fountain*"

On the Seawall: "At the Dealership"; "Without You"; "Practice"; "His Shaving Cuts"; "1985"; "Once in an Antique Shop"

Pensive: "A Showing of Acorns"; "On a Line by Charles Wright"; "Reading Revelation"

Plume: "On Reading"; "Hurdy Gurdy"; "Big Box"; "Whatever Alights"; "Morning's Only Yellow"; "The Bridge"; "The Cocoon"

Poetry Miscellany: "To Vincent Van Gogh in Heaven"; "Rainy Street, Portland, Maine"

Ruminate: "The Sparrow in the Banquet Hall"

Salamander: "The Recital"

Solstice: "On Ladders, Mystical and Otherwise"; "Bedtime"

South Florida Poetry Journal: "Thin Places"; "Galway"; "Crossing: Casco Bay"; "Talk Radio"

Upstreet: "A rabbi, a minister, and a priest walk into a bar"
West Branch: "Advent and Lamentation"

"Dear Sky" was first printed in *Balancing Act 2: An Anthology of Poems by Fifty Maine Women*, published in 2018 by Littoral Books.

"Thin Places" was reprinted in *The Orison Anthology*, vol. 5, 2020, Orison Books.

I deeply appreciate the people who have read these poems in progress. Many poets in Portland have had a hand in this book and I am more grateful than I can say. Thank you as well to Susan Aizenberg, Ted Deppe, Nancy Eimers, Sascha Feinstein, Lee Hope, David Jauss, and Leslie Ullman for your kind and keen-eyed reading of this work; and to Lee Sharkey, whose generosity has continued from beyond this life. Much gratitude to Sean Bishop, and especially to Ronald Wallace for many years of support. To my family: Through the darkest hours, you have been warmth and light.

1

There Is a Fountain

William Cowper, 1772

Climbing to the thinnest branch that will hold,
I must be more ponderous to the tree,
less musical than the birds I've scared off,
and less supple than the paper lantern I've come
to hang, to elaborate on a midsummer night.

I can hear my ancestors, not the leaves,
hissing "frivolous"—my people of the book,
of trees cut, shaved, pressed into pages of rules
warning against the mind branching out too far—
frivolous, that word easy to stammer,

so if I were on solid ground I'd stomp,
push it out with fricative force, though up here
I'll just hum to myself, looping a string around
the branch so this paper moon will cast its soft
unreal light, which, yes, the first drops of rain

could easily snuff. Oh, my flaw, my friend,
my stammering tongue, how I stumble over
your *ffff*'s and *vvvv*'s like a drunk, your liquid *llll*'s
that won't pour from my lips, as if words were rust,
woodblocks, wet wool, scotch tape, chipped marbles,

and why not? Why should it be easy to speak?
A flaw looked at another way is—I meant to think
a *source*, but it came out *scorch*. "So be it,"
my ancestors would say, those for whom
the body always betrayed the spirit's goal,

for whom the soul was a canary sent
into the world's mine, all mission, no pleasure.
They disdained ornament, as if to decorate
were to insult God. I don't know what they saw
when they gazed into wind-blown bristling trees.

It's a miracle that my ancestors actually
conceived, that all those overdressed mothers
gave birth. They wrote each name, weight, length
on one page of the book, our first words, steps,
baptisms on the next. But they were silent

when it came to delight, so we've had to find
our own way through dancing in the street,
drumbeat, dog romp, dock sway, one kind
of flaw or another, as limb by limb, up
from our roots, we teeter, we stray,

we find ourselves scorched, frail lanterns
on a twig's tip end where wood blends with air.
But there, with backbeat and blue note, songs
spill from our lips, they branch, leaf out from—
yes, our poor lisping, stammering tongues.

Big Box

Out here in the parking lot a young woman
stands blinking as her lover slams the door

and peels out. Book bag, short skirt, smudged eyes,
she stands on the yellow crosshatchings

and looks at her feet, as if staring down
from a high balcony.

Think of *King Lear*'s blinded Gloucester
listening to Poor Tom describe the lofty cliff,

the crows and choughs wheeling below,
the battering waves too far down to hear.

Or think how the actor who plays him
has to drop as if from a great height,

as if he weren't hurling himself hard
to a floor two feet below. Night after night,

how bruised he'd become.
Maybe he'd have to conjure the despair

or misplaced ecstasy of those jumpers
who really do leap from bridge or roof,

say, the ones who regret the instant after,
as if the air itself were a smack of hope

they suddenly remember. "Use your words,"
a mother says to the wailing child

she pushes across the lot, just as this
young woman's mother must have said to her

countless times—words that can name what she wants
and settle her down, words that can shape

a world that has nothing to do with this world's
real orbit and swerve, its fiery core,

and so she might come to feel they've betrayed her.
Still, to get through the night she'll need word

after word, till grief cries itself out,
and tomorrow begins to talk.

Practice

It all clouds, crowds back—my sister
hunched over the keys, cluster of notes
her hands can't reach or make fast enough.
She tries over and over that one tiny patch
of Bach pulled out from the rest like rubble
at the shore we poked through for treasure.

"If you are squeamish," Sappho says,
"don't prod the beach rubble," Sappho
who lived by the sea, soaking in its rhythms,
that first heavy wave shush hitting shore,
then the next softer shush and again, shush.
My sister shushed me over and over

as she prodded those keys, until finally
a cloud would burst, her fists would slam
down in a crash of sound, a wail of how
she'll never get it right, never be good
enough, it's too hard. But then the storm
would pass and she'd be trying again.

For years I heard only repeated pieces
like our old Evinrude refusing to start,
the choke not right, the engine not
catching, no sputter and shift into glide.
I had no clue what magnificent cargo
my sister was trying to haul, what was

inside the piano and inside her, depths
the ocean only hints at tossing up rubble,
fragments of Sappho, notes my sister now
lifts off the page, pours through her hands,
until if you didn't know you'd think
it was always easy, always whole.

The Daffodils

Daffodils, that come before the swallow dares . . .
A WINTER'S TALE

Either I wasn't thinking, or I thought
I could cross under the prison window
on my way to the town library and not be
a wound to those men, a flower to pluck.

My teacher intended no crime, assigning
the term paper on Shakespeare's *Troilus*
and Cressida, but enjoyed my discomfort
as he explained the racy puns. I found

Shakespeare guilty of not even trying
to make Cressida sympathetic, as if she
had been false for no reason but her own
pleasure—conniving, slutty, a pair of hips

sashaying past soldiers gathered around
their small fires—as if a girl with no
currency but her body wouldn't know
how thin the line between wager and ruin.

Memory's crime? The way it falters,
seduced by feeling, more fiction than fact.
Was there a walkway beside the prison?
Locked up long enough, a memory will

reenter the world hesitant, unsure.
Could there really have been open windows,

men calling out, reaching through the bars?—
young men, so not unlike these inmates

in my prison poetry class I've just asked
to make metaphors for the daffodils
I brought in. "Periscope up!" one calls out.
"Testing, testing," another says, holding

his fragile mic, and I don't know what
to say, when a third, as if taunted, pained
by the mute reveille of these bright trumpets,
asks, "Why are you doing this to us?"

On Reading

I used to think the things I read weren't real,
not as rain is real, or soap, or feta cheese,

that words in books were 2-D, like watching wind
through a closed window and longing to be swayed.

Despite having read it in a book, I wanted
"the wreck and not the story of the wreck."

Then out walking a country road one fall,
as goldenrod flared and apples dropped into wet grass,

I realized I was looking through a scrim of "mists
and mellow fruitfulness," and along the shore

I saw water "the color of mutton-fat jade,"
saw too in every museum, before every statue,

whole or hacked, what I wanted was the shiver
of "you must change your life."

And so I came to Augustine overhearing
a child in the next house chant "*tolle lege,*"

"take up and read," as God or the wind or his own
tearful anguish lifted child's play to prophecy,

words piercing his soul, real as "Zero at the Bone,"
as Whitman's mockingbird waking in him

"the fire, the sweet hell within" of love's longing,
which words woke me too, real as the water

that almost drowned me, as the shock of waking
on shore, sea-choked but alive—oh Jonah, Ishmael,

oh Granddaughter I saw the midwife draw
sleepy-eyed and small-shouldered from your mother's

spent body, and hardly thinking, heard myself cry,
O brave new world, that has such people in't!

Bear

Say you're out jogging in New Hampshire
and come across one feeding on berries,

too busy with those sweet juices,
with fattening up for winter, to bother with you,

who just wants to move along country roads
on your own two legs, between meadow and wood,

not too fast, not too slow, out for a run
before porridge. Innocent enough,

but still an intruder, still something a bear
might sniff as trouble, bothersome

to a creature intent on moving through
her world unharmed eating berries

with her cub on an August morning,
and so a creature much like you.

But there's that cub, and you've been warned:
sing, make a racket, till they shamble off.

A barroom ditty comes to mind,
all those bottles of beer on the wall, so you sing

as if a song could save you,
and wave your arms overhead to make yourself bigger—

or boorish, you might begin to think,
as mother nudges cub off into the woods.

After all, what did you see?
Just a glimpse of bear body through roadside scrub,

and nothing, nothing of her beauty.

Starlings

Nay, I'll have a starling shall be taught to speak . . .
HENRY IV

When my uncle grew obsessed with a flock of starlings
that messed the car he no longer drove at night,
I remembered reading how Shakespeare lovers,
hoping to populate this country with every bird
the bard named, had them shipped from England.

Whatever it says about us, not the lark, but these
creatures have thrived with their whistle and buzz,
spackled like doves that dove into tar pits and flew out
covered with road grit. They bully other birds,
tear up shingles, pry apart eaves. No matter

how my uncle shouted them off, no matter how
he raised his cane and railed, they came back
crowding the neighbor's suet with its greasy crumbs,
and because Shakespeare still hovers around so much
of what we see, I saw Lear in that old man's rage—

Lear, because he'd given all his worldly goods
to one lone daughter and then wanted to run her life.
Run or ruin: the two so at odds all she could do
was everything wrong in his sight while he fumed.
Now they're both gone, he of old age and she

of some failure or refusal to thrive, as if despite
three husbands and four children, without her father
the cigarette grit in her voice had nowhere to go,

15

without him no will, no stubborn intent to flourish
like these birds that even now crowd the churchyard

and forage among the graves, filling
the stony silence with quarrelsome squawks.
If they're such good mimics, let them pick up
the clatter of tags from passing dogs, sound
of those creatures father and daughter both

sank their affections in, speaking to their animals
what they could never say to each other—
Sweetie pie, *Good girl*—all the fond murmurs
dogs get the tone of, while the two of them heard
in the other's voice words they always wanted,

only said to another in front of them, so given
and withheld at once. So much *Never*, so much
stony reserve. Starling, I'd have you make
the sounds that once might have softened them—
dog sigh, tail thump, whimper at the gate.

Morning's Only Yellow

comes from the five sunflowers I bought last night
    at the grocery, their shade on this gray day
not quite *lemon*, but brighter than *mustard*—
    so many varieties on the color chart
(*olive, paradise, lion*), like the wines, cereals,
    cheeses, aisle after aisle, and varieties
of shoppers as well: two firefighters, a young couple
    counting their change, a drunk lurching
among juices, mumbling to a small girl strapped
    in a cart with her doll, watching her mother
read labels. At the store's dairy end two men
    wearing muscle shirts and leather vests
strode in, one holding a newborn cradled in his arm
    like a football, swinging it back and forth.
The infant was half the length from elbow to wrist,
    still in his blue hospital cap. A woman
in slippers shuffled behind, and I followed to see
    what would become of that child.
(Had they biked here, a sidecar for mother and baby?
    Would a hospital release a child to that?)
At the checkout the firefighters' two-way radio
    squawked. The little girl was using
her new word, *lellow*, to point out to her doll
    the lemons, bananas, Cheerios
her mother put on the counter, and nothing else,
    as if what she couldn't name she didn't see.
What I couldn't not see was that man
    swinging the baby as he gestured
toward bread or beer. Heavy boots, biker belt—

the opposite of *tender*, I thought,
and so had to worry through the dazzle
    of aisles, our bodies in slow forage.
But in the next checkout lane the baby slept
    while the men piled their 12-pack, diapers,
toilet paper and chips on the belt. His head
    didn't roll and his arms didn't startle,
so he must have been held with more care
    than I could see. Maybe he'll be nothing
like the boy next door, who after school wanders
    the yard tossing pebbles at his house
until his mother opens an upstairs window
    to curse and threaten the belt. He turns
then to his sister, as if he can't bear to see
    her cradle her doll, singing, *baby, baby*.
Has to grab it and race through the yard
    while she weeps. Has to threaten to toss it
over the fence and sometimes nearly does.
    It hurts to think what he wants and can't say
is to be that doll in somebody's arms, rocked
    until his fists loosen, his eyelids drop.
Lellow, lellow, the little girl sang her one word
    for all the shades. Shades or words—
do we ever have enough? *Amber, citrine, marigold*;
    tender, delicate, lenient, supple, frail.

Thinking of Jonah at the Children's Museum

Zipped inside a nylon whale, breathing air
pumped into that fishy tent, hard not to think
of Jonah, sorry and scarved in seaweed,

hard not to picture the ship receding,
huge watery acres of abyss, breakers
sweeping over. And jaws, the tight squeeze
through baleen, stew of stomach acid . . .

Until then, easy for him to not want
Nineveh spared—no TV image to show
funnel or mushroom cloud, barrel bomb

falling on market stalls, hospitals, schools,
on children like ours now in the pretend
grocery paying play money for empty
cereal boxes and wooden apples. Jonah,

like any self-declared judge and jury
justifying jihad, Jim Crow—until, cast down,
cast off, banished from the living, shut

inside the jail of himself, he cries out.
And does he hear the whale sing its eerie
God-speak, like wordless Jehovah in high-
pitched echo and reverb? After which, he's

hurled, as if he's just stumbled from a club
after how many volts of trumpet or sax
have jolted through him from some quartet's

live socket, stumbled out, all circuits blown,
no sense of who he is, where he's from, no calling
down judgment on another soul. So much
unknowing—what would you call that? Joy?

The Recital

Because the final piece ended with the organ turned off
but the keys still pressed down,

there was a rush of air, as if the whole church exhaled,
all of us part of that great stage whisper.

Applause would have jackbooted the room, scribbled all over
the sounded silence,

so people gathered their coats slowly, nodded to one another
and moved toward the street still inside that swell,

an absence of sorts, but how to speak of the way it made
each gathered-up scarf, each object our eyes fell on fully present?

When the doors opened, a group of students walked out,
then lingered on the steps arguing about art—

a magnificent ruse, or the only way we have to move
beyond ourselves into something larger?

As they went on, I waited in the back of the church,
watching the organist gather up her scores and speak politely

with the few who couldn't bear to let her go
without somehow touching the source of that sound.

I watched, almost surprised to think: This is my sister
changing her shoes, shutting the clasp on her portfolio.

I say, "my sister," though surely she was born on a different star,
pulled with tongs from a different furnace, already glowing

with a passion to pour herself into sonata and fugue, Ligeti, Bach,
to stretch her fingers on every chair back and table edge—

so much music inside her she had to expand her reach,
test every surface to see which ones were willing to be played.

Soon we too were down the street, eating Chinese,
chunks of pineapple, green pepper, cashews and pork,

recalling how we skated in our socks across the blue linoleum
of childhood, dreaming oceans, horizons beyond

the confines of our mother's widowed house.
We remembered how in our ordinary earthbound past, the one

in which magnificence had nothing to do to us, my sister
wore braces and broke her wrist, had a boyfriend

with a sailboat big enough to enter open sea—a catboat,
so with far less rigging than the music she had just played

with its long spar, its many sails, ropes, crow's nests, mysteries
sealed in the hold. She laughed at that description,

and because it was late and we were full of billowing music,
good fortune and wine, we started flicking our invisible cigars

and Groucho-striding across the midnight street, happy
to be sisters and small inside a world too big to fathom.

Hurdy Gurdy

Like a grumbler who claims a five-year-old
could paint a Jackson Pollock,

I'm out of sync with this club's special guest,
who's set up in a half-walled alcove.

His "hurdy gurdy" is no little fiddle-shaped thing,
but a huge electronic console with wires

and switches, all making a tuneless drone—
sound of tires hitting the rumble strip,

buzzy mutter of cartoon ghosts in a wall,
trapped there among the batting and slats.

The man turning the wheel, twisting the knobs
doesn't even try for rhythm or song.

He wears a wizard hat, so it's easy to think
he's toying with us, making us listen

to this noise with no arc or purpose or end.
And I do want it to end, want sheetrock and studs

between me and this inscrutable mumbling.
Maybe my ancestors are ghosting me,

those four-square types who didn't even like
Sinatra coming in a single beat behind the band.

And Elvis? Oh, shudder! It must be them in me
this noise unnerves, the way it mocks, saying

lyrics lie; melody's a made-up dream of order;
the world's a chaos box of static and squawk:

Make up meaning, if you must, but it won't be true.
On and on it goes, this rhythmless din,

as if it's the sound underpinning the world—
what we'd hear if we could really quiet down.

"Without form and void," the Bible says,
before God separated light and dark,

the first wall: Chaos on one side,
shape, meaning, music on the other, the words

I'm putting to the scratch and groan of this machine,
while it's feeding me the need.

The Birthday Party

Ferry Beach

The hand of God, on the lips of a bikini'd woman as she trudges through the sand with a friend, could be wind, or a burning tree, a stranger brushing her shoulder, or maybe a kind of answer to the boy, newly ten, who's just asked if being a grownup is hard. What to say? Even the history of these stones, tossed by waves and now skipped across them by the boy, may include fire, ice, crushed ferns. So little is straightforward. First the kiss he gave his mother, then his squirm out of her arms, back to the water. Whoever said love isn't complicated, if he wasn't a fool, must have passed through some burning gate found only by those who have stopped trying to grasp or explain. How to tell the boy none of us, when we agreed to breathe, crawl, walk, read, knew the journey would not reveal itself in advance, so our best maps are dreams, Escher-like roads that dissolve, then reappear, looped through tilting scaffolds. But never mind, never mind. Now the boy's mother photographs the sky, slant of clouds rippled and glowing, a sermon in which awe overwhelms uncertainty, and dread has no place here where low tide reflects the splendor overhead. Yes, the sky will dissolve its radiant path, as if to say looking elsewhere is not the answer. *This* will turn into *that*, cake into crumbs, bright wrappings into balled-up trash, and yes, it is hard, but there are gifts, Child, gifts. You among them.

2

Dear Sky

I stood on the library's seventh floor and there you were,
enormous in its bank of windows, no longer squeezed
between buildings, filtered through leaves.

Above the tree line, I was eye level with a gull
skimming past and four pigeons in ragged formation
who circled round once, then disappeared.

How present you were, how *here* and *full*—
densities of bubble wrap, feathers, silk scarves!
To the south, ink thinning through water,

a thickening roux to the west. Is it true
one cloud weighs as much as an elephant?
How easily *cloud* becomes *could* . . .

The child makes you a blue inch at the top of the page,
and it's still hard for grown-ups to think you come
all the way down to the space between grass blades

and the sleeping drunk's nine unbroken fingers.
Liquid, yes—and gas—but in what form
do you touch the mother at the border wall,

her milk gone and the child still hungry?
What tenderness or chill gets her, weary as she is,
to rise, bundle the child, and keep walking?

To the birds you must be one indivisible country
as they fly Canada to Cancun—you who can't be
leveraged or foreclosed. But damaged, yes,

damaged for sure, the soot of you, the shock wave.
How to look at you without seeing ourselves?
How to even conceive atom, eon, dust

drifting down from your glowing bodies
to be part of our bodies, the light and dark of you,
inscrutable cloud script, invisible link?

A rabbi, a minister, and a priest walk into a bar

and in that brief gap before punch line,
how many thoughts run through your head—
preachers of abstinence come to shut down
the joint? three men losing their religion

in gin? paragons of morality
holding hell over our heads while they pick
our pockets? Could they be three *anythings*—
undertakers, doctors, English profs?

Or does the joke need that long history
of wars, pogroms, Pales, need to recall that
a minister, a rabbi, a priest once
would not have been funny at all,

given the old murderous urgencies?
But now, to meet at day's end for a drink,
for friendship and inside jokes—it all seems
so tame, some will think it's the end,

while others just the beginning of faith.
Some will say love thinned to nothing,
others that it's finally grown deep. "God
only knows," one of the three might sigh,

and raise his glass. So, *a priest, a rabbi,*
a minister walk into a bar, and—
of all the ways it could go—*the bartender*
looks up, says, "Is this a joke"?

On a Line by Charles Wright

"God is the fire my feet are held to,"
   he writes from his yard in Charlottesville—
and first I picture, not marchers,

   but my father's black-and-white world,
his walls and gates to keep everyone in place
   going up in smoke and charred soles.

Today the sun turned its back on us,
   leaving snow, rain, deep slush in the road,
so cars whoosh by like monster angels,

   slashing the air with huge transparent wings.
Such a heavy sky, low, a winter white,
   not even close to the color of my skin.

Who decided to call us white, when we are
   clearly a pale beige version of the rich
gleaming dark we came from, watered down,

   as if that makes anything pure? Get over it,
my sad brothers storming hateful
   and hoodless through town. Read Dante

before rage makes you gnaw your own flesh,
   leaves you glaring under burning muck,
flakes of roof, rebar, smoldering cars.

If you don't like to read, give a listen
to Thelonious Monk, his tunes seared clean
   and spare, hammer and hesitation. The way

he fingers the keyboard, you know it's true,
   The piano ain't got no wrong notes.
But it does got under and between notes,

   over notes, bent, blending, got Monk
playing not *sorry* but *wake up!*
   So maybe the flame God holds our feet to

could be cool—if we'd toss in our old lies,
   my brothers, your *them or us*—if you saw,
my father, how they're burning us up inside.

Ladders of Paradise

Rung of boredom, rung of daily distress
  from morning news, I thumb aimless
through my phone, landing on a twelfth-century
  icon, *Ladder of Divine Ascent*, with rung
after rung, monks on the rise, some falling.
  A bigger screen shows more—
a huddle of figures at the icon's bottom edge,
  hands folded into prayer, and at the top
what must be saints leaning to yank a monk up
  over the last arduous rung. Outside
the wake-up stun of a blue jay's shrill,
  then from a tree near the feeder, his song
like a punk rocker pulling a flute from his back pocket.
  Rung of beautiful bully scattering sparrows.
Last night after dinner with friends, after hugs,
  sweet rung of fellow-feeling, I stepped into
the street's blue dusk, and there at a sidewalk table
  was my old boss, rung of resentment,
how in a band he'd be the horn player
  hogging the mic, the one who splits
when it's time to pack up. But now no title,
  no desk, no deciding vote, no classroom
to set up with the prettiest girls in front. Small,
  sunk into himself. Handed me his card,
said, "Write to me, send a question for me
  to answer. Ask about some trope."
And so this morning, rung of reluctant pity,
  I saw I could have done it, didn't have
to toss the card. But what would I ask?

Not about tropes. Or maybe exactly that:
ladder, rung, rise, fall. The little wobble
    from my weight testing the first step,
iffy shift as things settle into place,
    then the short climb to prune or pluck.
Do the monks give all this up, one by one,
    rung of hunger, of earthly pleasures,
rung of nursing old wounds? Scary
    how almost at the top, threshold
of whatever bliss is, even there one falls.
    Not much hope then for earthly ladders,
say, ambition's crowded steps where those below
    rush the heels of the ones above,
till somebody stomps on fingers, somebody
    kicks whoever grabs at their ankles.
So many ways to fall. And to rise—
    is there just one way, straight lines,
right angles, or is that group bunched up
    at the icon's bottom also headed
for paradise? And what about this tree
    jutting out in every direction, rung
splitting into rung, rising, improvising
    by crook and bend? And here's
that jay again, rung of skittish and brash,
    spiked-up crest, his many blues,
from smoky to bright ladder-back of tail,
    the way he flies off, then in the leaves,
that penny whistle, that flute.

Once in an Antique Shop

What in a baby's mind allows her to laugh
before she has what we think laughter requires,
language, outlook, irony? But here she is,

in this crammed and dusty shop,
twelve weeks old, in her mother's arms
and laughing. The land may be coming

apart, warring lawyers, legislators, landlords,
and not-so-latent fascists hard at work
undermining everything we stand on.

But the baby ripples all over and laughs
as her mother changes her diaper, then
settles her gently back into her pack.

Around us an overpriced Coca-Cola sign,
a nicked and gouged wooden dough bowl
somebody will pay big money for.

What the baby doesn't know delights her,
and her delight almost reaches me
as I finger a piece of Civil War lead

that may have passed through a man's liver
then lodged in a tree—gouged out when?
and by whom? carried in what pocket?

for how many years?—to end up here,
where this baby gurgles and stretches her limbs,
grinning up at her mother from a world

without irony, where she is not separate
from anything she sees, a world before
like and *lie* and *loathe*, and so she laughs

in her great unknowing, as though she comes
from a place she hasn't yet forgotten, a place
where such knowing doesn't need to exist.

Missing Person

Does my voice sound like wind blowing across
a glass rim? Strange that I even try to speak,

here, where rust has unhinged the sign, so it hangs
by one chain banging against the shutter,

tavern I hurried past on winter nights after closing
the library, avoiding the men

who spilled onto the walk. What made
the streetlights flicker made me want to be invisible,

as I truly am now, just a breeze, a ripple of snow—
not a series of called-out body parts, not a target

for grunts and terrible gestures, not a name
phoned into Missing Persons after three days'

absence from work, and no one at home to notice
the hungry cat, the wilting fern. Passerby,

call it bad luck or fate, but an hour earlier or enough cash
for a cab and I wouldn't have entered that storm

of spurned, laid-off men, bitter and raw.
Had I the barmaid's sharp tongue I could have

talked back, kept them teetering on their heels, at bay.
But thick glasses were all I had,

sensible shoes and an armful of books between me
and the rough-edged world I thought I had left behind.

I was a fish in a barrel for those hands,
that sour breath, those taunts like hot pokers.

Then something else like that, only worse,
until I bled out in the back of a truck

and was tossed in the woods by men who swore,
sober, they could never do such a thing. Passerby,

if some idle stroll sends you down another street
where wind stirs an eddy of cinders or tugs at your coat

it could be me, a timid woman past her prime,
or any number of other women, men, boys, or girls

in all the colors and shapes of flesh, who had our last breaths
torn from us. It's not a need to be heard

that gives me voice now in this swirl of snow,
but the way the world is—filled to overflowing with us

in the haze around streetlights, the invisible dust
filling the air. Stranger, no telling what anyone sees

in the end. The very thing I sought to leave behind
is what I saw as darkness closed in—

billowing sheets, nightclothes, pinned-up socks
crisscrossing the old tenement yard, line after line,

and sweeter than I ever knew, the pulley shriek,
as hand over hand, a woman slowly reeled them in.

A Showing of Acorns

In this little thing I saw three properties. The first is that God made it. The second that God loves it. And the third, that God keeps it.
JULIAN OF NORWICH, *REVELATIONS OF DIVINE LOVE*

They don't have wings, so only fly when the wind's strong, fly then fall, bounce a little when they land. Their hats have no straps. Children draw eyes and mouths, so they have faces, but no ears. No legs or arms either. Thalidomide babies. Like my schoolmate Bill with his one leg, who'd windmill down the long college hill on his crutches, whistling as he flew. Such an abundance that year too, such abandon and dance, a great undoing. Day and night they ping on car roofs, clutter the sidewalk. Cars park and drive off, park and drive off, filling the gutters with a coarse meal. For hands the surgeons made Bill a set of pinchers so he could grasp pencils, button his shirts, hold a racket, and sometimes gently squeeze my shoulder as we stood talking. This morning an acorn struck me on the forehead as if to knock in a little enlightenment, or to bring back Bill, whose last name I can't recall, though he was made and loved and therefore, beyond me, remains.

Ugly Beauty

The piano ain't got no wrong notes.
THELONIOUS MONK

Out of gospel, out of big band, out of whites-only
dance floor, out of backdoor entrance, relentless feds,
out of piano jammed in kitchen doorway, diapers on top,
out of work, out of boredom, out of other and more
and unspoken, comes not fusion, but fission, comes
melody split into echo and off beat, stutter and dodge,
and still listeners leave the club humming. But what
would we have to know to speak of him? Who flat-fingers
those keys into percussion. Who, over the ballad's steady
drum brush, pecks out piano notes one at a time,
then a flock tumbles down staves. Scatter and land.
Bird foot and wing. Ugly Beauty. Wit in the darkest times.
Sheriff Clark blocking marchers on the Pettus Bridge,
while Monk crosses so many, up and down the keys.
Who ground his teeth into sharp jagged tunes. Beauty
of stumble and lurch. Surprise that doesn't grow old.
Skullcap and shades. Pinstripe, beret. Wisdom mumbled
as if it'd be happy to stay inside amusing itself. A/muse. A/maze.
Ugly Beauty? Keyboard plowed up like good earth, roots
deep in the word "alone," as if the god particle hid inside,
mixed with a storm slosh of chemicals, tipped off orbit.
Takes his pay home. Takes the rap for a friend.
Leaves the stage to call his wife, lets the phone dangle
from the wall box and plays so she can hear. Yes,
he inhabited the twentieth century. Yes, he changed
the meaning of time. Of course he was always late.

Does anyone know what he suffered? Yes, a genius,
and yes, jazz, pronounced dead, returns like skeptics
to God, prophets kicked out of church, hitting the street.
Those who have ears . . . The fifties finally ended. The world
didn't. Same old promises, posturing. Same dark suits, white
shirts, red and blue ties. Ugly Beauty. Meaning the notes
try on every change they have, seersucker to dashiki,
and a man's a genius to sound like himself.

Bargains

Listening to Robert Johnson—"Dust My Broom,"
"All My Love's in Vain"—you can see how
the stories got started, the crossroads, the pact.
But can you imagine wanting something so badly

you'd sell your soul? Maybe you wouldn't
believe in souls, or you'd think you could
out-trick the trickster, and at any rate
the debt won't come due for a long time.

Besides, the devil gives you what you want,
at first. Johnson gets that uncanny voice,
those guitar licks, juke joints, train rides,
applause, invitation to Carnegie Hall,

plus liquor, women, until—well, until
what—poison? syphilis? His body found
on the side of the road in Mississippi
where no white coroner bothers to examine.

And where to pay respects? Three different graves
bear his name. Easy to wonder if a pact
with God would have been better. Except,
who can bargain with God? Ask for skill or fame

and you may end up asking so long you find
you have made a life without them, singing
and strumming each night to the cockroaches
and your landlady banging on the door.

But you might get good that way, good enough
for roadhouses, rent parties, Sunday church.
Maybe late in life someone comes round
to record you playing, now through broken teeth,

swollen knuckles, a frayed voice, playing
as if the grass at your feet, the road dust,
the cottonwood trees and every body
that ever hung from one were there, deep

inside your fingers, your throat. Their lives,
your art—who can tell? What if the devil's
last trick was supposed to erase Johnson's voice
from even the slightest waver of air, but God

stepped in and swiped those records right out
of his bony hands? Not the devil's music
after all, but the sound of a soul fully spent,
down to nothing left but raw joy, grit and hum.

Everest

On the musical scale of vowels, *E*
is up there at the level of shriek.
Eeek, a mouse! Seek is one thing,

Eureka! another. So much searching
for ecstasy, endless satisfaction,
as if you could stay on Everest forever.

"Third heaven," St. Paul talks about
in one epistle, though how he got there
he can't say, and he can't stay there either.

The thorn in his flesh, whatever it was,
made sure of that. As my love says, you can be
so heavenly minded, you're no earthly good.

Easy to imagine enlightenment
belongs to just the few who scale the top,
or those high-flyers who thrive on extremes,

and not the little guy down below,
not the monk walking home from the river
with his bundle of reeds, but the devil

who stops him to brag, "I do all the things
you do. You watch, and I never sleep.
You fast, and I eat nothing at all."

Happy, Happy, Happy

Keats calls the figures on the Grecian urn,
never arriving but not dying either,

as if we're always on the road *Between*—
truth/beauty, head/heart, heaven and earth—

or what was that recipe we found once?
Himmel und erde, mashing apples and potatoes,

so the two we loved separate were fused,
like healing stirred, blended into hurt,

till they can't be told apart—the wound,
the tear, the break that lets in light . . .

But I thought *happy* meant arriving
at the goal, then getting to hang out poolside

after hard work, sipping a pastel drink
with its little paper umbrella.

Who wants to be stuck going round and round?
Still, if you're Keats spitting blood,

or the bull on that urn, then the slower you go
the better.

It must take more than dragging our heels
to arrive where Catherine of Siena does,

saying all the way to heaven *is* heaven,
especially when it looks like hell: the hacked-up

ruins of what once was a town, the heavy weight
of the dead loaded onto carts,

the buttons, bones, shoes still in the rubble
when survivors comb through.

Against these scenes, only the smallest gestures
seem to hold—the cup of water

handed to a prisoner on a train, the shawl
wrapped around a shivering child at the border,

the last piece of bread a hungry man
breaks in two.

Slow Night at the Piano Bar

Dear left hand not doing much on your end
    of the piano, can't you run a little ruin
        over the rhythm, break out of your stride?

Dear fingers long and slim, reaching out
    of your cuffs, please shake yourselves loose
        of this steady stair climb and get down,

put a little feeling in those felts. Dig the black
    and whites. Spotlight on your brow's sweat says
        there's more inside than anyone knows.

Play it. Bring us to our knees. Help us
    forget what we came here with, our solo selves,
        secret weight and grief. Put a little leaven

in the lines, pile up the notes till they outrun
    our thoughts, enough keys to heaven it must
        be everywhere. Unlock us, loosen our grip,

so we turn our pockets inside out and blow
    our inheritance. Be the match that lights
        our pyre. Dear sinister second string,

shadow side, left hand lagging behind, forced
    to hold back in favor of the right, please
        drop what you've been lugging around,

let yourself leap, riff, rough up the tune,
   till it upends, lifts off and carries us
      somewhere in our right minds we wouldn't dare.

Thomas Merton Experiments with Meditations on Jazz

Abbey of Gethsemane, April 1967

It starts with Jimmy Smith swelling the B-3,
    his music welling up out of those keyboards
as the Hammond's liftoff fills the moment
    like a small forever, however long it lasts.
And for that, thank you to the great chain
    of witnesses: to Smith himself, to Merton
for recording his call and response, urging
    the music on, to whoever gave this tape
to the DJ who then compiled and mixed the show,
    and especially to my friend Ted
who sent the link that's let me hear the sound
    of a man losing his life, which scripture says
we must: lose, loosen, let go, enter the music,
    its eruption of vitality ghosted by pain,
as Smith works his mojo, pulling out stops.
    And then to whoever listens, Merton reads
from the Book of Jeremiah: *"Your work will be*
    rewarded . . . There is hope for your future."
April, 1967, the earth grinding on,
    mixture of hope and dread, cities in flames.
The subject of his meditation, Merton says,
    is who you identify with, is Smith pouring out
soul, organ blazing, throwing off sparks,
    black power in those chords; the subject is
the future still reeling through darkness, is

all things turning, the record, the tape, that mojo
working, the earth still here, still backlash,
    still these prophetic voices—and still
the monk says, *Got a choice who you listen to.*

3

The Cocoon

Visiting my cousin's church I found
the preacher charming in his depiction
of the apostles flying by the seat
of their pants, Holy Ghost shirttails:
Not knowing a blessed thing, Brothers
and Sisters, but alert, just looking
and whizzing around—Imagine!

So it was easy to take my sad self
to the prayer line and let him go
hammer and tongs, hands tight
on my head: Unlock, open those
mighty floodgates, let inspiration
roll, let it pour down— But then
he just stopped, stepped back,

said he had a word for me straight
from the big guy: Don't touch
the cocoon. But, but, those floodgates—
what happened to them, that surge
gushing out? I wanted to ride that
rush like a water park slide, not get
some crappy inscrutable word.

The minister grinned. Bird bait,
he said: That's what you get
if you open a cocoon too soon.
That critter has to strengthen its wings.
And how does it do that, my dear?

Elbow and nudge, it shoves. Amused,
he looked at me, one brow raised,

as if he could see four states away
me back home, muttering to whatever's
bigger and beyond, as I jog the steep
hill by the milking parlor, then down
the farm road, past the placid cows,
the open field, muttering about want,
always wanting to break out, be free

of my uptight, my don't-have self,
whatever form it takes on any
particular day—grievance or need—
and do I even see the monarchs
and viceroys drifting over roadside
milkweed, unperturbed by my passing,
by the farm dog's bark and growl?

Reading Revelation

The dog wants a walk and I want to close
the Book of Revelation, to step out of locusts
and woe, even if it was Dickinson's favorite.

Imagine those brassy trumpets, vials of poison,
scorpions, horsemen, there, alongside dough
rising in her Amherst kitchen, her pages

of wildflowers carefully labeled and pressed.
The quiet life's shadow book? Night text
for opening the furtive mind?

But boiling seas, drought, flames, infestations—
it's such a big production, *Ben Hur*,
Moses, and all the *Star Wars* combined.

Here it's spring. Sidewalks finally clear,
we walk freely, not mincing our steps,
no more black ice, puddles of snow melt.

The dog's happy to be at this small pond
where hidden in reeds bullfrogs belch and twang—
creatures, not symbols of foul spirits,

but real bodies, mud-mouthed, mysterious,
with their bass croaks and bubble eyes,
their almost-man legs camouflaged in slime.

A car passes wearing a bumper sticker
that asks, "What kind of gun would Jesus buy?"
And I think somebody will answer that

with serial number, model, and make—
a real gun, not a poet's loaded metaphor
or scripture's "Turn the other cheek."

In Dickinson's noisy bog, she's glad to be
nobody. But my mind's already veered
to those big somebodies, presidents and generals

high on empire, tossing people like dice,
till it's hard to imagine the world set right
without conflagration's total delete.

Still, the dog rolls in grass, happy and meek,
the frogs call for mates with their throaty songs
as passersby push strollers, jog and ride bikes.

Somebody tell me what would it mean
to want, for the sake of a new shiny world,
this world and all that's in it dead and gone.

On Ladders, Mystical and Otherwise

1

After my neighbor's stroke his ladder
leaned against the same cedar tree till its feet
began to fray back to the earth they came from.

What pruning was left would stay undone
while the ladder remained, as if someone
hoped he might come back to reclaim it.

But now the roofers' metal extension
shrieking up the side of the house shakes me,
sound the dead might make who've been gone so long

they've put down roots, seeped into the ground—
sound the dead roused by Hieronymus Bosch
for the Last Judgment might make, yanked up

dangling tendrils of flesh. Hard to tell
by their looks who's going up, who's headed
back down. Not a happy face among them.

2

More than once in a country church I have
heard a buzz of voices, the choir singing,
"Let Me Take You Higher," the minister

wiping his brow, someone shiver-shaking
in the aisle, as the congregation is swept
up above bills, bunions, and hard thoughts.

We must be on that invisible ladder
mystics speak of, rising golden above
gravity and grief. But the faithful know

there's also a coming down, hands empty—
no buying or hoarding in this house.
There's the drive home and what might happen

on the mountain road's hard curve, its glare ice.
There's the radio with its heartbreak news.
Always the journey, not yet arrival.

3

Imagine, before the wheel there were ladders
so far back we can't know who made them,
how erect or hairy, how verbal, how fierce,

or what wanting they worked into this tool.
A tree's honey hive too far up to reach?
Or was it down they desired, a cliff's

hidden nest, small recess, below which waves
dash against rock? Either way, like bees
something buzzed in the brain—maybe the same

longing that led me as a kid to lug a chair
up to the shelf where the forbidden sweetness
was hid, my own risk of teeter and fall,

some wanting that's hard to shake off,
hint of pleasure flickering, and that longing
to rise, or raid whatever's out of reach.

Meanwhile, the mystics warn: climb too high,
too fast, and we're bound to fall. Like that
cartoon critter on TV rushing up rung

after rung, as each one splits underneath him,
until he's climbing on air, then—*oops!*—looks down,
and like St. Peter suddenly plummets.

4
Maybe we don't talk about *down* enough,
where some of us get sent, ready or not,
that rag and bone shop, school for soul-making,

where a friend ended up drunk in an alley,
having just learned his heroes were fallen—
famous theologians he had supposed

were above the sleaze of dark desires . . .
Son of a suicide, that young divine,
always looking for fathers, often betrayed,

found one he didn't want in a drunker drunk
who scooped him up as the snow thickened
on his shoulders and got him verbal enough

to say where he lived. For years he lived on that,
grounded, sober—the father who got him
to his couch, then slid back into the night

to possess the alley, father he couldn't grasp,
was too drunk to see, but he remembered
the stench, the smelling-salt reek that woke him.

5

My friend says we shouldn't call Jacob
a sleaze. But he was on the run, he did
stiff his brother. Not someone you'd think

would see in a vision that ladder stretched
to heaven with angels like bees bridging
the distance. Still, no easy rise for him.

However an angel or God wrestles,
who of us in our own torn souls, tossing
through some dark night's dread or regret,

couldn't learn from Jacob holding on
until that blessing comes? And with it as well
a hand to his haunch, as if to say—

but isn't that always for the seeker
to figure out, like Jacob alone, deep
in his flesh, feeling with every blessed step

that hitch, a hinge ringing in the bone?
Like walking a prone ladder rung after rung,
ecstatic or penitent—either way, stung.

6

And so we go back midweek for prayer,
climbing out of our cars, up the church stairs,
some with canes, or needing an arm, a kind word

to rise out of the day's sweat and sorrow,
just one rung, maybe, but enough to see
over whatever's blocking the view,

to ask for a glimpse, a hint of something
above or beyond, a little heaven-honey
to ladder us up as far as our minds

or hearts can go—into the spring trees
where branches fill with such sweet buds
the bees busy themselves in those blossoms,

shivering with pollen on their legs, passing
the peace from flower to flower, the sweetness
increased, the honey nothing until it's shared.

After the Keynote Address, the Drive Home

The app said to follow Route 16 to Route 4,
but 16 turned left and became a lesser road,

barely two lanes, curving through empty fields,
past tilting barns, silage wrapped in white plastic.

No houses or shops. Nobody to ask if the road is right
or if I'm lost. Nothing to do but go on

till I come out somewhere far from podiums and applause.
My companion, Thelonious Monk, plays his musical lurch,

trying to think something new with his slow climb,
hard landing on one odd note, listening for other times

inside the time we keep, for what's underneath
the melodious *smooth*. Yellowing fields,

high-crowned road with its endless dip and rise.
Trump signs, double lines, a tractor that won't pull over,

so mapless, with a useless app and no cell tower,
I think even the aliens have packed up, signaled home:

Don't bother with earthlings; they'll do themselves in.
Meanwhile, piano comping two saxes, then suddenly chimes

like musical rain or beaded curtains opening up
a quiet space inside the space I thought I was in.

And now a crossroad's blinking light,
a burger joint that looks more closed than open,

but full of regulars hunched over the counter,
who make me a stranger with just one glance,

then nobody worth a second. Still, here I am, landing
on this creaky floor in dim light through greasy windows—

a nobody wondering what nobody's hungry for,
watching a fly step carefully over fork and spoon

to make my acquaintance. Sheer wings, marvelous eyes,
Are you nobody too?

Bedtime

My granddaughter, to put off sleep,
wants to talk. About what?

Flashlights. So I begin
with batteries, sizes, degrees

of brightness. But she says,
No, no. You're just talking *about*,

as if she knows the writerly advice:
present, present.

So I begin again: What if
you could choose the color

and wave the world yellow or blue?
What if flashlights had magic batteries

to make the sad people happy,
small people big, somebody smart?

Or if the little circles they make
were baby moons the big moon

could lean down and kiss?
After which, she rolls over,

Goodnight, and that's that.
Only I'm left lingering in the dark

having puzzled all day over Job,
hardly able to make out

the difference in all that talk
between him and his comforters

and God. Except maybe all the others
are talking *about*—their spurious

theories that the good thrive,
the bad suffer, and God is big,

yes big, but there are rules . . .
Until out of the whirlwind,

out of cloud swirl and hoarfrost—
suddenly there's no about, just *Is*.

Downstairs in a kitchen drawer
I find a flashlight and move it

across the unlit room—
droopy boots left by the back steps,

fat aloe plant with its pulpy spikes,
dark gleam of the oven door

where things inside
get transformed.

Thin Places

Home now and jet-lagged, we're up too early,
the sky still black, the time somewhere between
Halloween and All Saint's—a thin place

our friends called it, driving from Connemara
to the airport, a place where borders between
the living and whatever's beyond loosen

like masts turned to wavering lines in water,
or the world outside rippled by old window glass.
Maybe it's just our need to think we feel

something brush past, an almost-heard voice,
the hard fact of death suddenly fluid.
Or maybe it's we the living who lay down

our defenses against the dead, their demands
and disapprovals, their wounds that wounded us.
In Dante's Paradise everyone's transparent,

reading each other's thoughts, as if all need
to hide has been sloughed off. His great hosts
appear in waves of light gentler than the waves

we watched all week through our friends' window
as the North Atlantic threw itself down
against rocks, then fanned up in spray, wave

after wave, the glass a kind of thin place
between us and the water's wild crashing—
glass itself neither liquid nor solid,

but something between, amorphous,
like the dead still moving through us, their genes
passed on, their passions and fears.

Last night children dressed as wolves, gorillas,
witches, and bandits knocked on doors asking
for sweets, as if it doesn't take much

to tame our shadows—less than a lifetime,
less than an afterlife working off what's bent
or blocked inside us. Across the street now

houses emerge from the dark like vague hulks
as our windows grow transparent again,
no longer glossy like the inside of waves

before they topple. Soon light will fill
every space between limbs, porch rails, trellis—
shadow and light, inseparable sea

and shore, living and dead, everything touched,
as if boundaries are thresholds after all,
the way even solid rocks wobble

in the waves, even the hard, shelled creatures
stuck to those rocks, barely alive it seems,
open themselves to the tide and drink.

Elegy with Bats

Austin, Texas

They poured out from under the Congress Avenue bridge
as twilight came on, first a few, then like a dam bursting,

dark figures plumed through a darkening sky,
bits of ash billowing up to *thousand* the air,

as Dante would say—like memories of our sister
swirling around us. She too had darkened in the last years,

so we strained to recall all of who she was,
her quick mind, her fearless missions, fierce beliefs,

teacher and human shield—before stroke stole her thought,
and she became for us not unlike the bats, half-seen,

swarming in jittery clouds. Our sister, so quick
to fix a problem, fluent in Kierkegaard, Sartre,

Spanish and French, on her last visit had shrunk down
to opinion's endless sputter,

wanting the last piece of toast, first cup of wine,
the talk focused on her, annoyed by a tree out front,

insulted by sunflowers next door. *Stupid, stupid, stupid,*
she stomped past those bright yellow petals, bonnets

brimming each round face. She hated the ones bent over
like dying Christs slumped on their stems.

Pathetic! she said, as if anger were the last ember of self
now without sonar, flitting, aimless, amok—

until at the end, our niece said, she was silent, her gaze fixed
on some unknown world no one else could see

any more than on that bridge, as the bats dispersed
into the deepening night, we could discern

when the last one had flown. Still, we lingered,
our eyes adjusting to shades, densities of dark,

as if we could see where a last breath, a life goes,
a soul cut loose from the body's tether.

We stood in a crowd of others, locals and visitors
like ourselves, lingering in the summer night,

the heat of the day finally gone down with the sun,
which had, I reminded myself, not gone down at all.

It was earth that turned. And there, on the bridge,
the crowd thinning, I had to grasp the rail for balance,

as the thought filled me: the earth actually spins
day after day in space, no visible string, no pedestal

or base to hold it, nothing but that turning,
and the weight, the sweet pull of other celestial bodies.

Transmigration

Question: What do you want—the journey or arrival?

Love's body? (Love's arms, back, hands, tongue, thighs—)

Then what?

> On the bus home from the airport, after your stepfather's
> ninetieth birthday, you sob into a cocktail napkin,
> What's the point?

> All those mornings rising at 4, all those numbers, contracts,
> meetings, reports, only to end up shuffling, frail.

But: of such good cheer.
After the rooster years of strut and crow,
to have grown tender, open . . .

> Late sun slants across high-rises, burnishing them as the bus comes
> out of the tunnel.

> The flare of roadside trees, a few leaves, sun-struck yellow—
> flicker of wings, or notes on staves, "melodies . . . unheard"?—

Could that be enough?

What is longing—to belong? to be poured out? filled?

To know? Or to give up knowing and be
known?

       Night, the bus window darkens, your face a smear on the glass,
       your thoughts all nudge and shove,

Oh, little monarch, admiral,
your thin wings, the long passage—

Corcomroe Abbey

Twelfth century, County Clare

When we arrived at the monastery, a guide
was midway through his talk on ruin and dates

as yellow birds twittered past window holes.

We wondered if the ancient holy ones
stopped trying to be good and just sat or kneeled

astonished by the birds' antiphony.

Of course, we too came here
hoping to be cracked open, amazed.

Before the roof fell in, before the grass

made itself at home, the monks must have
bent over their texts:

Condemn not, forgive, give—

words that might save, or simply shimmer
like grass blades in late sun,

solvents for hunger and dread.

When the tour bus left, taking its information,
the stones settled back into silence,

not so much ruined as struck real by the light.

The Sparrow in the Banquet Hall

Story first told by the Venerable Bede, 673–735

I'd ask the sparrow why its nature is
to hide from me—if it even noticed,

if I weren't a late arrival on earth,
long after the little bird learned to love

the deep recesses in thickets and leaves,
the supple give of limbs.

As for the deep recesses my kind knows,
there are stories we call history

about all that is lost in tangles of the past.
From centuries ago, there's the sparrow's

brief flight through the banquet hall—
in one door to all that's warm and bright,

then so soon out the other, and back
into the long winter night,

meaning where we come from,
where we're going, those great unknowns

about which the angels say, *Fear not*,
but only after we have fallen to our knees.

So many new words for those unknowns:
big bang, black hole, light year, dark matter—

as if they tell us any more,
as if all our loves aren't married to loss.

Truth is, when a heartbreak song comes on,
before it swamps me, I turn the dial.

And I don't want to know if the banquet ends
in a brawl, wolf dancing on the table,

or what happens to the king and his thanes.
Oh, angel-dressed-in-your-sparrow-clothes,

I lean over the small pond beside your thicket
as my face breaks into ripples

like visible static and then dissolves.   ·
Is this what I'm supposed to *fear not*,

what you've been saying over and over?
I look away for just a second

and when I turn back—
where have you flown?

Galway

All day we walked, from Salt Hill along
the wind-whipped bay, in and out of rain and pubs,
Spanish Arch to Nora Barnacle's blue door,

past a sandstone list of famine ships, and as if
even travel were a test, I worried we might
come and go unchanged, unthrilled, ungrieved—

throwback to my family's creed, its endless need
to *measure up*. The English side, that is.
The Irish were all dead, so couldn't sass back

asking, *to what?* A crane, a mound of iron scrap.
Coal tits, hooded crows, swans. A fragment of
medieval wall, beside which toddlers played

on a plastic slide. End of day, a squall
scurried us into St. Nicholas, with its alcoves
full of headless figures leftover from hatred's

iron pikes, gargoyles and graves nearly effaced,
stone floors gouged, the locals like to say,
by Cromwell's stabled horses. There, the Irish

must have risen in my blood, so I saw:
Too much ruin and wonder for any measure.
A candle then. We tipped ours to the flame

of another burning on its wick and joined
that little skittish family of light.
Walking back later that night along the bay,

against the wind, we were glad to be in gusts
of rain, happy to be soaked and buffeted,
in our yellow slickers flickering.

Whatever Alights

A zillion yeses to the titmice at my feeder,
to their silky gray backs, their white bellies
tinged in rust, their little black eyes.

Yes to the fruit and nut mix that draws them,
to the runner who scares them off, the nuthatch
who comes back first. And yes to my sister

suddenly back from the dead as if from Austin,
calling the bird silly for the way it spirals
along the tree trunk upside down.

And—why not?—yes as well to her taking
the last of the cereal, the wine, retelling
the plot of her novel, memory's one door

she can still open. After years of being smart
in four languages and dumb in the dialect
of feeling, years of *so what* to the birds

and *how stupid* the crepe myrtle, she's back,
gentled, and because a woman, she sings
as I fold laundry, songs from Cameroon—

she who worked hard and grudgingly for God
as if God were more chore than marvel,
she who divided the world into like

and dislike, useful, useless, broken, fixable.
I wonder if on the other side of the river,
that Rio Grande only the dead can cross,

the birds are no longer nervous, the air
free of predators. When she returns
my sister no longer limps, hardly grumbles

or says *stupid* when really she means *sad*.
It's as if she is back inside our mother hearing
the soothe of muffled cadences before words,

before yes and no, whatever hurt her,
whatever alighted and then, before she could
hold it, flew or was snatched away.

4

Knot

That's Dante's metaphor for what he can't
    unravel: how to square a good God
        with a suffering world, or slip free will
into the master plan. . . . For us it's memory,
    whether it shapes the self, or the self
        shapes it—*your* self, Love, that bright mind
now finding its threads loose and tangled,
    so the man at the door—will you know him
        to be your brother, or for a second
stand there feeling frayed? *Self*—how we're trying
    to hold on, baggage and all, like that gorgeous
        visiting professor, her three suitcases
for one weekend, who said when we drove her
    to the airport, "You don't think this look comes
        easy, do you, Honey?" It made us wonder
how she looked undone in night's solitude,
    who she was then—who anyone is.
        And on our visit with relatives last year,
when my sister and I both confessed
    we thought the other had sucked up all
        the attention, so we each felt left out,
you laughed, asked how she and I could both
    be outside wanting in, said it was more
        like we were each behind a closed door,
and only had to open. Sounds easy.
    But open to any knock, whatever path
        is laid before us? Dante walked through

terror and ice, then a wall of fire,
    and one river to drown his memory,
        another to bring it back cleansed
of bitterness and regret. Then for him—
    Paradise, his whole self swept up, lost in
        love's brilliance. But here on earth
the light that falls is knit with shadow,
    bringing a darker knowledge: the two of us
        bound in knots of love and grief
            we couldn't, if we would, untangle.

At the Dealership

The morning paper they've given to distract us
grieves for eight bikers killed on the road
and an airport bombed in the Middle East.

It welcomes new refugees from Angola
to our small city, which has opened
the sports arena to offer housing.

A friend texts that she had a sleepless night
and feels weepy. My love, for whom reading's
grown difficult, opens a *National Geographic*

to wild animals used to draw tourists,
then hobbled and caged, pangolins killed
almost to extinction for their scales.

Our daughter puts a photo on Facebook
of herself at three, in jeans and cowboy boots,
so young I almost weep at that bright face.

Salesmen bring good news for some,
big repairs for others. The rest of us
check the time, settle in. My husband

turns the page, and there's the Sargasso Sea,
itself turning like a slow gyre,
surrounded by four currents and no land.

Around us a businessman phones in
to change appointments, an elderly man
cups his ear to catch his wife's words,

a young woman scrolls through her phone.
On the paper's front page, people stare at a sea
of cots, having traveled far and still not done.

A pod of whales is held in small filthy tanks
in Russia, whose language my husband
once spoke, he for whom our daughter

waited each evening on the porch, dancing
as he pulled in the drive, he who could change oil,
rotate tires, whatever the car needed.

How strange to think of a sea without land,
the doldrums of little sleep and long waits,
the way we grow porous in stalled transit,

endless currents of longing and grief.
When it's finally our time to pay
I ask the manager to roll up his sleeve

and show us again his tattoo—
five stick figures with smiling heads
and small waving hands, a drawing

his children made for him and he's had
inked on his arm so he can carry them
as long as his arm exists.

1985

After the supercell passed through, we were
stopped at the crossing, the dog and I,
watching the train's cowcatcher stuffed
with green boughs. Uprooted trees blocked
our route home, sent us down country roads
where radio towers blink all night, warning
whatever flies: turn away, don't soar into me,
don't be the moth seduced by a light that kills,
by that ultimate longing to merge. And yet,
what night didn't I drive toward light, toward
warmth, sloughing my coat at the door?

◆

I could pick any year, say 1985.
What happened then? Say I jogged the cemetery,
past storm-downed trees, uprooted sycamores
and oaks, then home into welcoming arms.
Say the world wanted only calm vanilla skies,
a vanilla president, and turned away from
darker sorrows. Say in a church basement
I worked the can opener around the huge tins
of government meat, while another woman
stirred it into something edible for those
coming in from doorsteps and alleys.

◆

Say there was a man in a black choir robe
with plastic spoons pinned down the front
like military medals. And a young woman

whose pupils swirled when she spoke of outer
space, as if she thought that to study the stars
you first have to burn, lose yourself in light-
years until you can't find your way back home,
and so drift through shelters and soup kitchens
among men with the scent of booze oozing
from their skin, with deep pockets in their coats
for cradling their bottles of moth-light.

◈

At the end of the night, we'd send them out
into whatever storm was brewing, while
inside it was trash, scrub bucket and mop,
then the drive home stinking of grease
and sweat, home to warm arms, bright eyes,
and children wanting a story, a shirt
ironed for the next day. Oh, in 1985
were we too busy making it all happen
to ask what it meant? Though really I knew—
it was those arms at the end of the day,
and children I could feed kisses and stories.

◈

It was the men and women at soup kitchen
wanting to tell someone how they spent their day,
a whole table of old women wearing white gloves.
In 1985 we got day-old everything from various
stores and concocted edible meals, and no matter
how many men peed on my tires, I got home
to lights, the door flung open, to lingering arms,
children, the dog wagging, and most of all
to the bed where I'd lie down beside my love,
the way he'd chuckle on the verge of sleep
as if entering a sunlit realm after rain.

One Step

Who am I to say to the man: You can't
sleep in corduroys and a dress shirt,

or: Don't stick your fork in the potatoes,
spoon them onto your plate,

as I must have said more than once
to our children.

To the man I would have said: What does it
mean to be saved, and from what?

Or I'd ask about a friend's blunder: How can
somebody so smart do such a dumb thing?

And he'd half smile, then shake his head:
Don't you understand, it's not about brains.

How can I tell this man: You can't sleep
in anything that has a leather belt

or a wallet in its pocket, and: Here
are your pajamas, which he puts on

inside out so the flannel pockets flap
like limp fins and he laughs

and flutters them awhile before we start
again, right foot in right leg.

He laughs too at my schoolmarm self,
asks: How did you get so bossy?

Me, he once held through months of sorrow,
who without him might never have swum up

from those dark waters. Who am I now
that he is longer that man, and we

are something other than we ever
imagined? Saved, he would say,

in part from ourselves, whatever in us
is grasping, fearful, controlling.

Into what? I'd ask, and he'd roll his eyes,
knowing better than to answer.

Or he might say, as he did more than once:
Into gratitude, my dear. And: One step at a time.

As now, left foot into left leg.
And: Here is your night shirt, I say.

Do you want help buttoning?
Not yet, he says. Not yet.

Advent and Lamentation

Many summers the goldfinches came,
the sunlit dozens of them, early and late,

a bright twittering as they swooped
down and teetered on the clothesline.

We felt blessed by birds, chosen,
and I still don't understand why

they found other feeders, other souls
to lavish themselves on, leaving us

dry-docked on our scrap of yard
yellowed by dog pee.

Now a drubbing of rain on car roofs
and trash cans, so I imagine neighbors

banging pots and pans, chasing off
some poor squatter or any drenched soul

who's got to *walk that lonesome valley*—
song we first heard from old-time fiddlers

on our friend's Appalachian porch,
autumn-brown mountains all around,

a place we went to visit, then lived
seven years, walking that valley, yes,

but it wasn't lonesome then,
though clearly the song said it would be

and now is—first my love's lonely Covid bed,
then me without him. How that song smacks

like a skylight collapse, cloud thrash
mixed with shatter. Dirt-finch, mud-light,

world-stop. If just for one minute I could see
radiant floorboards, a door blown open

as something blazes in, burns right through.
Mary, mother anonymous, is that how it was

when the angel-gust broke in, that gold-wing
speaking Seraph to you, and you were

all *Yes, okay*, even then going griefward?

Without You

First time I listen to Thelonious Monk
without you, the recording we left in the car
that ends with the band working out a tune,
the start and stop of it before flow, Monk's
voice coming as if from beyond the grave.

I saw graves from the church parking lot
where I waited to meet our friend M
to walk her new dog you've never seen,
10 pounds—you'd chuckle, the way it runs
on short legs like a windup toy.

First pretzels I've eaten without you—
leg cramps, so our son said they'd help,
the salt, which people called me in contrast
to sweet you, which must be right, given how
mosquitoes passed by me to swarm you

as when I first took you to the ocean
where we kissed, until you started jerking,
slapping your arms. Weird. But then I saw
you were getting bitten, so we left
and resumed kissing in the car. First time

I thought of that in months. People say
memories console, but without you?
All those jazz ballads I can't listen to
without you. First food binge, chocolate,
even before I got home from the store,

and later too many pretzels as if I ate
for us both. We were such a both,
watching movies on the couch, our hands
meeting in the popcorn bowl, so we'd grab
fingers and kiss awhile, then have to rewind.

Our granddaughter texted pictures of frogs
I looked at without you, thinking how you
would have belched, made those *rib-bit* sounds,
and bugged out your eyes, then said what a good
photographer she's become. I took a chance

and walked to the pond where we'd listen
to frogs. But it was nearly dry from drought—
no dragonflies, no lily pads, just soggy leaves
on the bottom, black muck, green algae scum.
See what's become of the world without you?

Widow, Walking

I don't want a day when I never think of you,
but I would like more in the morning news
than another briefing on your absence.

I miss hearing my name as summons to a kiss.

If we can't step into the same river twice,
with the past it's not even once.

Memories are hot watches, knockoffs
pinned to the insides of my coat.

I open it and become a flasher.

At least the wind is wild today, the trees
in a frenzy. If I wore a wig it would be
long gone, snagged in the crook of a tree,

but good for containing something
that starts off fragile, then grows wings.

If you are a spirit now, can you hear me
or have you left our flesh too far behind?

Somehow I've landed at the shore
where late sun makes the seagrass glow,
and for a second I don't want to hold you

or anything, not moonrise in the east
or sun gleam in the west, not the path
of watery light washing my feet.

Still, I can't stop talking to you. Grief

is a heavy coat, dragging the ground.
But death is very cold, so I wear it.

The Bridge

After the cortisone shot the doctor said
    take it easy. But the bridge was just
        beyond her office and I needed beauty.

So go ahead, she finally said, but slowly.
    Before the water, on the embankment:
        goldenrod, coreopsis, Queen Anne's Lace.

Some kind of party last night, humans first,
    then gulls: a litter of cellophane scraps,
        barbecue chips, peanuts, sunflower hulls.

The tide was rolling in with the wind, three terns
    (I think) dipping down, catching things. Clover,
        tall grass, smashed mussels, dried seaweed.

Because my hip still ached and the shot needed
    to settle in, I walked slowly, took my time,
        and Dickinson came to mind: "I started

Early—Took my Dog—And visited the Sea—"
    Which seemed to stun, overwhelm her.
        "He—" she says, "He followed—close behind—"

And I thought *you*, how often we walked
    this bridge. I'm not the first woman
        to grieve, to need the tide and open sea

beyond the dull ache of you now gone.
    Cracks and glitter mixed in the concrete,
        sharp shadow of grass heads, perfect replicas.

All those ancient journeys the living take
    into the afterlife to embrace a shade,
        to grasp, and grasp again only air.

There was a breeze that wasn't you, you
    weren't the tide, didn't rise to meet me,
        you weren't the dandelions on the bank,

the light, the shadows, the broken shells—
    unless to see you at all I have to see you
        in everything, first bowing, then withdrawn.

Talk Radio

You'd think the battery would run down
as the man, having sanded, now paints
my steps, just one side today, so I can
come and go, and the mail be delivered.
But the voice gets so worked up, it seems
about to loosen the hand brake, roll the car
into the gutter. It sputters and fumes,
feminazi, *bitch*, as if it sees the woman
passing with a sure stride. A Black man
out with his dog gets spewed on too,
verbal exhaust: *12% of the population—*
who cares? If I could put a paper bag
over that radio, smash it, stuff it with
a sock, anything to stop the yammering
know-it-all barking from my handyman's
car. This blast-mouth—does it believe
what it says, or just say what sells, and sell
whatever we're buying? My handyman
checks his work, touches it up, his back
to the radio cranked so loud the whole
block has to hear, even my neighbor's
St. Francis who stands so still real birds
land on his head, Francis who said, "Preach
the gospel. If necessary, use words." It's
not words my handyman offers, but arms,
when I tear up, saying once my husband
would have done these chores. So, now
I have to wonder in what compartment
of himself does this man put the radio's

rage, its audible spit, have to see in myself
the part that would tie it up like a sack
of kittens and toss it into the river, the other
part that waves as the man drives off,
stands on my steps half painted, half raw.

Crossing: Casco Bay

He is not here to walk this bridge with me,
    to pause midway at the rail and gaze

at the water's dull glitter, the many islands,
    and between them passage to open sea,

not here for me to quote Whitman saying
    to ferry crowds, "Just as you feel . . . so I felt,"

or to tell about my childhood ferry
    leaving Camden to cross the Delaware.

We'd be going or coming from funerals
    for great-uncles and aunts, there'd be talk

of the dead sailing toward an endless horizon
    no one in this life can reach,

that distance where the light is so brilliant
    it hides whatever's behind it.

"Distance," Whitman says, "avails not,"
    imagining himself gone, crossed over,

and still reaching out. After the bridge,
    there's a causeway propped by landfill

and boulders, studded with shells dropped
    in the night by gulls. Goldenrod, asters,

sumac, lichen, some kind of netting to hold
        the rocks in place. How often we walked here

holding hands, and now in his absence
        I want to believe distance avails not,

as if a soul really could sail out and cross back.
        "You furnish your parts toward eternity,"

Whitman says. But what do the living know
        of those currents and tides, that light,

the gleaming road I watched from the ferry rail
        making a path straight to me

and saw still when I stepped to another spot,
        so knew it was there for anyone who looked—

the far side of the horizon, vast reach of open sea—
        there, and yet I fathom it not.

To Vincent Van Gogh in Heaven

After the gunshot did the crows scatter
or swarm? If heaven has a gate,
is the latch on the inside or out?

You with your bandaged ear, just the lobe,
not the whole rose of it deadheaded,
as I first thought. You who can make

the tamest flowers wild, make any field
stubbled and lush, dizzy with lilies
under the stars, and on my way home

from walls hung with your sagging boots,
plowed fields, lumpy potato eaters, sunflower love,
make everything on the street a bright shock—

first the rut and peel of a door's blue paint,
then the thick bark of trees, and the glint
of my dropped keys under the streetlight,

one sad, whose lock is long forgotten,
two with sockets they still fit. And now rain
washes the street taillight-red, caution-yellow,

rain that kept you inside wild-eyeing
your room and remembered gardens, inside
your troubled head, the yes and no of you

doubter of everything you did, believer too,
saying, Heaven, hello and good-bye
and may I come in? Vincent,

may I call you that, because I crave
your gouges and grooves, your paint so thick
it's more real than the drenched iris

under my window. Because your skies
pulse with such abundance and abandon,
I want to believe even in anguish

you turned a knob and the lock sprung,
the doors flew apart, snapped their hinges
and still hang loose on their jambs, and open.

Rainy Street, Portland, Maine

Painting by Brian Killeen, 2017

It must be between State Street and High,
    perhaps the block near Port City Blue,

music club offering Saturday night jazz.
    Rain makes the sidewalk bricks glisten—

but aren't those walks really concrete?
    So in this way the scene's imagined,

an artifice of pattern and form, the salmon brick
    reflected in storefront windows,

contrasting with varied blues of awnings, autos,
    and one lone figure out walking

with a long watery reflection.
    Despite the rain there is a lightness

to the sky, as if it's about to clear.
    We bought this painting in December

at a friend's show, you and I
    each putting down our bank cards

so it could be our gift to each other. Now
    it fills the wall, wet blur of street

and that one figure carrying a blue bag
    doubled on the storefront glass.

Gazing, I'm aware of being warm and dry
　　while also recalling the chill of rain

as we headed out to that club,
　　where some nights we found ourselves

almost outside of time as flute, guitar,
　　bass, and drums took us far

from the tune's melody into pure attention,
　　the air alive with improvisation,

so immediate we both leaned in as if to touch
　　some almost mystic source.

Perhaps the painter also leaned in,
　　making quick improvised strokes,

starting with a photograph, then choosing
　　the colors, blurring things

to make the feel of rain and expectation,
　　order and uncertainty,

something about to break open,
　　the way those nights there'd be the stun

of flute or guitar riff, or later a full moon
　　as we left the club.

Now you're gone, but you left this gift,
　　your half of it, the way it seems

half of everything is you—your kind spirit,
　　wise words, keen eye.

I look again and see a touch of green—
    signage above a shop, and another figure

on the sidewalk nearly blended into what
    might be a mailbox behind it, a figure

revealed only by its reflection on the wet bricks.
    How often have I gazed

and until now not noticed this ghostly blur
    merging into everything around it?—

this thin ripple of presence almost pulsing,
    whether it's walking toward me or away.

The Caterpillar

What does it know when it eats and eats,
turning leaves into dried-up lace,
or a teenager's hole-ridden jeans?

When it spits out thread and wraps
itself tight, does it know it's going
to decompose and be transformed?

Or is it just wound up in itself, wound
and wounded, shut blind in its own dark
as if hunched over on the therapy couch

held rigid or falling apart in sobs,
not knowing anything can ever budge,
that there is an outside to step into?

I asked my love why he kept
in his office a green cloth caterpillar
hand puppet he could turn inside out

to untuck bright silky wings. For a child,
I assumed, but he said, No—for anyone
passing through pupa, falling apart

or needing to let go. I never thought
to ask how he used it. Maybe it was
just there, all potential in that room,

as it is now here without him,
plush parable of a creature having to
let go everything in order to change.

Miserere Mei, Deus

Gregorio Allegri, 1582–1652

I didn't mean to find myself here,
where first the tenors lay a foundation,
then the sopranos raise up rafters
impossibly high, a cathedral built

by voice alone, where I didn't mean
to be kneeling, to be lighting a candle
and wondering how mercy got put in
a word that sounds more like misery—

a cathedral made of air, so my prayer
is like calling to the future before
it appears: Are you sure you want me
to step out like this, putting on grief

like a secondhand coat, so much heavier
than it seemed when someone else wore it?
I didn't mean to keep entering this music,
vault by vault, built by the sweet brevity

of those high boy voices breaking the heart,
until who wouldn't cry out in surrender?
Naves and ruins, bodies turning air
into soul, space for grief and desire

here in this predawn hour glowing blue
where sorrow is gathered up into the words
of a psalm, stirring the marrow,
nudging until I am willing to toss

myself like bones into the future's pot,
willing to say, *Yes*, oh secret heart,
as the sky lightens, *Yes*, to the mercy
that only comes when misery cries out.

His Shaving Cuts

His shaving cuts, his big brow bones,
that quick smile. He stands in the doorway

under the skylight in a freak shine of sun,
snow-bright. The whole city is blinded,

shovelers out in their shades on every street
bend and toss. Dangerous pavement.

But not to him. Schoolboy grin, bits of tissue
stuck to his cheek, he's thinking: no work,

snow day, and where are my gaiters?
Then a quick kiss and out the door.

Shush of his skis gliding down the street
past the stench and groan of snow blowers.

Where does Spirit live? Can it be held
in language, in giddy words unhindered

like the twittering of birds—not rules,
but joy, where I see only work?

This kind of breaking and entering
I can take. Him stepping into snowshine,

even if it so welcomes, so blazes around him
there's no way back.

Notes

"On Reading": The lines quoted come, in order, from Adrienne Rich, "Diving into the Wreck"; John Keats, "To Autumn"; Elizabeth Bishop, "The End of March"; Rainer Maria Rilke, "Archaic Torso of Apollo"; Augustine, *Confessions*; Emily Dickinson, "A Narrow Fellow in the Grass" (1096); Walt Whitman, "Out of the Cradle Endlessly Rocking"; and William Shakespeare, *The Tempest*.

"On a Line by Charles Wright": The quoted line is from his poem "Ars Poetica II," *Appalachia* (Farrar, Straus and Giroux, 1998).

"Everest": The quoted passage at the end comes from Thomas Merton, *The Wisdom of the Desert* (New Directions, 1960).

"Thomas Merton Experiments with Meditations on Jazz": This poem derives from the experience of listening to "The Jazz Monk" on Indiana Public Radio, April 12, 2017, compiled and hosted by David Johnson. Thanks to him and to Ted Deppe for sending the link.

"The Bridge": The Dickinson quotes are from "I started Early—Took my Dog" (656).

"Crossing: Casco Bay": The quoted lines are from Walt Whitman, "Crossing Brooklyn Ferry."

WISCONSIN POETRY SERIES

Sean Bishop and Jesse Lee Kercheval, series editors
Ronald Wallace, founding series editor

(B) = Winner of the Brittingham Prize in Poetry
(FP) = Winner of the Felix Pollak Prize in Poetry
(4L) = Winner of the Four Lakes Prize in Poetry